Conquering Penang Property Market

A Real-Life Experience of
An Engineer

Derrick Jonathan

Contents

Preface 1
1. How I met John 7
2. Unravel John's secret 23
3. Return on Investment 35
4. Acquiring 10 Properties Within 5 Years 53
5. Biggest mistake: buy and stay 69
6. Make sure someone pays off your debts 83
7. Follow the game rules 93
8. 200% ROI within 5 years is not a myth 107
Epilogue 121
About the Author 125

Preface

Property investment has been very tough after 2008, especially in Penang. After property price significantly soared from 2008 to 2010, housing price was increasing at a moderate pace. Many speculators got burn as they don't have enough holding power and were forced to auction their units and some of them even have to declare bankruptcy.

Property has been everyone favorite topics during luncheon or gathering. Most of the time, those topics were open-ended. "Do you think the golden era has passed?", "When will the property price decrease to give us some bargains?", "I believe it is time to buy." Those are all common questions which even the wise one cannot answer. Nevertheless, are those really something we need to pay attention to? For those who succeed in property investment, those are unlikely their main concern. Their main focus is to develop their own plan and stay in the game for the long term. Market fluctuation always exists. The only difference is the level of impact. You may have small corrections in every two to three years and major corrections in every ten years. Why worry on those rainy days? Stay focus, acquire property which will be your golden goose.

This book will open up your mind on property investment. It is a life lesson of an engineer based in Penang who able to acquire more than 10 properties within 5 years. It sounds astonishing for some of us; it is also very difficult for me to digest when I first heard it. Yet, after I followed John's little secret of investment, I greatly regret not knowing John earlier. John is an engineering manager in one of the Penang semiconductor company and a successful property investor who live below his mean.

He just turned 35 years old, and he likes to run. Consistently, he participated in the Penang Bridge run every year. He drives a 4 years old Honda City and stays in a new condo which cost him about RM600,000. He married 4 years ago with no kid, but he lives a happy life with her wife. At least he has one thing less to worry about: struggle on getting food on the table. He is a minimalist and always emphasize on keeping good habits. He has his goals to achieve every day, and he consistently stays in his routine. 1hour reading, 1hour running, 1hour investment review, 1hour spending time with family, remaining hours working in the office, sleeping and also stuck in Penang congested traffic. On the other side, I am also an engineer working in Bayan Lepas Free Industrial Zone. I graduated 7 years ago and will get married a few months later. Although we are tight in cash, we purchased a similar condo as John did. Since then, John and I have become neighbors. He is nothing difference compares to us. He goes to work at 630am, knock off at 630pm and most of the time, stay at home after that. It is when we have dinner together that we unravel the secret which John is holding.

He is a very successful property investor. It greatly surprised us when we get to know that. I am very sure you won't be able to sense it too. He used to wear a t-shirt, short pant, and slipper for almost all occasions except going to work. To fulfill our curiosity, John is kind enough to share us how he did it in the past. He told us that he made a plethora of mistakes in the past and he should be able to do even better if someone can provide more insights to him before he gets started. While we were following his life lesson, we did not recognize the wrongdoing, and it seems to be the right thing to do at that moment. However, when he pinpoints those mistakes, we finally able to recognize them.

In this book, with inputs from John, we will discuss the secret to acquiring more than 10 properties within 5 years. In fact, it is a very simple strategy that everyone can follow. Many of us have the wrong perception that only the rich can acquire multiple properties and grow richer. That's not the case most of the time. No doubt, it is definitely easier to kick start if you have more cash on hand. Nevertheless, the amount of cash you have will determine your starting point. You will still be able to be successful in property investment. Having said that, if you have limited cash, you will have to start with lower cost properties and progressively moves up till you are able to acquire higher end properties. It will take you more time to reach the peak, but definitely not a showstopper.

If you can acquire the knowledge and skillsets that John is deploying, you will definitely shorten your time in becoming a successful property investor. You will learn through the mistakes and successes from John. All you have to do is to avoid repeating those mistakes and duplicate whatever John is doing. However, I have to warn you that this will be a long-term process. If you are looking for fast money, you will be disappointed with what we will discuss later. However, if you are practising the concept consistently, in the longer horizon, most probably 5-10 years, you will be greatly benefited. Your net worth will increase, and you most likely will be financially independent or financially free. In every chapter, we will share John's experience, and the lesson learned thoroughly. It will be interesting to read, and it will be eyes popping sharing. You will greatly benefit throughout the journey.

1. How I Met John

I graduated from University Science Malaysia in 2010. I was extremely lucky to get to know my wife during my university time, and our relationship is going very well until now. Just like everyone else, we wanted to have our own apartment. In Penang, our elder one always told us to acquire property earlier as the property price will only go up. If you purchase in a later date, you will end up paying more than supposed to be. As we have those thoughts embedded in our mind, most of us start to look around when we accumulate sufficient cash for down payment.

Thanks to the lower property demand in 2014, my wife and I were able to acquire new property with a very minimum down payment. This new property is located at Sungai Ara, Penang. We were amazed by the mountain view, windy and quiet environment. It was our very first unit; we spent hours discussing the pros and cons before we finally made our booking. We even went to inspect the area for more than ten times. We talked to a similar salesman for multiple times till the salesman attitude changed from good to bad.

Finally, we placed our booking as we like the quiet environment, low down payment and it is still within our budget. We always wanted to get a luxury apartment which we can have a small getaway every day when we reach home after work. This new development sounds a good buy ro us because it offers some luxury facilities with affordable price. There are a few options to choose from. There is pool view vs. city view, high floor vs. low floor, with balcony vs. without balcony, three rooms vs. four rooms and small unit vs. large unit.

My wife was really hoping to get a better unit and almost entirely forget about our budget. She was proposing to have a higher floor, pool view, and a larger unit. I was more focus on the budget. I argued to go for moderate size, city view, and low floor unit. The price is about RM10K to RM20K cheaper for city view unit, RM5K extra for incremental floor and the average selling price is about RM500 per square. If you are going for the 30th floor, pool view and 1,400sqf unit, you will be paying approximately RM700K. On the other hand, if you are going on the 10th floor, city view and 1200sqf, your cost is only about RM500K.

After some debates, we finally agreed to buy the 18th floor, city view, and 1200sqf unit. It cost us about 560K in total after rebate. The attractive part of this project is the high rebate at down payment. We were given 8% down payment rebate, and we only had to fork up 2% down payment to own 560K unit. That was only roughly RM12K. Additionally, they offered vouchers which are able to offset most of the interest payment which we have to bear before the apartment development completed. In other words, you own a RM560K condo with only RM12K down. A good deal for us, especially when we are limited in cash and loan eligibility.

We waited for almost three years until we were informed to collect our keys. More than 10 times, we purposely passed by the construction area to inspect the progress. We also followed closely on the updates posted by the developer on their website. In April 2017, finally, we collected our keys. We were delighted, and we even went out to have a nice dinner to celebrate. However, we totally forgot that we have to liaise with contractors to renovate our units and to furnish our units with good furniture. We didn't even allocate enough money for both renovation and furnishing.

After some thoughts, we finally decided to look at whatever we have and budget ourselves on both renovation and furnishing. Meanwhile, we have to complete everything by the middle of 2018 as we plan to get married and we need a home to stay after our marriage. We opened up our saving book and looked at the figures. I have saved about RM25K for the past two years while my wife did only about RM10K. Our base salary is almost the same, but she spent more on dressing herself. With RM35K budget, we are really limited to what we can do. We decided to budget our renovation to RM25K and furnishing to RM10K.

To lower down the cost, we go to a contractor who provides the cheapest quotation, and it was only about RM23K. We gladly accepted the deal, and he promised to start renovation by June 2017. At June 2017, he postponed the construction work to August 2017 and postponed again to October 2017. We complained multiple times, but it was useless. I guess that is the reason why his charges are low. Low cost, high quality is most of the time a myth. It took him two months to complete everything. The workmanship is not very good, but it is better than what we expected as we really have very low expectation.

Once the renovation completed, we used our remaining RM12K budget to furnish our unit. As the budget is very tight, at the end of the day, we only able to furnish living hall, dining hall and master bedroom. Wherever that we don't think we will spend much time at, we will just have left it empty for that moment. Once we have more budget, we will fill them up.

Once everything is completed, we are ready to move in. we moved in at Jan 2018. We left most of our heavy items at our rented apartment nearby Queensbay Mall. While we were moving our items to our new unit, we noticed that our opposite unit was already occupied. It seems like they have moved in for quite some times as we don't see much boxes which we normally used for moving items outside their unit. We wanted to say Hi, but their door was tightly closed. We thought about doing that maybe in later date or when they open their door.

As the condo is still very new, the occupancy rate is still very low. At Feb 2018, the occupancy rate is only about 30-40%. Although we stayed there for slightly more than a month, we never meet our neighbor before. I guess everyone is working very hard and we depart and knock off at a different time. One day, I was working very late as I am rushing in developing presentation materials for tomorrow meeting. I knocked off about 7:30pm and arrived at my apartment around 8:15pm. Right after I parked my car, I finally saw our neighbor. I greeted him politely, and we started our very first conversation.

"Hi, I see you parked your car just right beside me, I am guessing you must also be staying at the 18th floor," I asked happily. "Right, I guess you must be the one staying opposite my unit. My name is John" he replied. "Nice to meet you, John. I am Derrick. I always wonder when we will meet up, it has been more than one month since I moved it" I said. "Absolutely, I believe it is because you are working extended hours today, thus giving us a fate to meet up," he said. "Are you saying that you always came back about the same time?" I asked very curiously. "You guess it right, although my official working hours are 8am till 5pm, I normally stay till 700pm before I make a move. That will help me to skip the terrible traffic, and in the meantime, I can do some reading or finish up my never-ending tasks" he replied.

"I have to keep going, my wife is waiting for me at home" he continued. "I see, you are staying with your wife? Do you have any kids?" I was reluctant to let him go and insist on asking more questions. "You know what? We should just hang out when we find the time. Here's my number, let's get in touch" he replied impatiently. "Alright, sure. Let me WhatsApp you also. Let's keep in touch." I replied.

Since then, our work became very busy. We can hardly find time to have dinner together. Finally, after one month, we were able to spare some time to get to know each other better. As we might want to talk quite a bit, and the weather is extremely hot, we selected an air-conditioned restaurant which is less crowded and less noisy. It was a Japanese restaurant located at Golden Triangle at Sungai Ara, Penang.

"Finally," I said. "Yeah, you are right, finally" he agreed. "How's work?" I asked. "Don't ever mention" he replied. We laughed, and we made a promise not to put work-related topics on the table. "What do you think about the unit you are staying now?" he asked. "I think it is good. It is less noisy, unlike what I have experienced when I stay nearby Queensbay Mall. It has very good facilities, although I have not used any of those. The only disadvantages I am seeing is poor air circulation and too close to the next apartment" I complained. "But, I have a very different opinion, the unit I am staying is very windy, and I have very nice mountain view for now," he said. "I guess that is because you have pool view unit which is RM10K-RM20K more expensive" I explained. "Wait a minute, why do you say you have nice mountain view as for now?" I continued. "I guess you have not heard that the similar developer is planning to build three more high rises surrounding the mountain?" he explained. I was shocked, and in the meantime, I feel fortunate as I don't pay extra for mountain view which will change to concretes view soon. "You really should drop by my unit after dinner to make a comparison. I think you might regret not paying extra." he insisted. "Sure, love to do so" I responded. I am very sure that I won't regret it, but I am also very curious to look at his unit. Windy and nice scenery is not something I can imagine now.

It was about 8:30pm already. We quickly finished our dinner and met up again at John's unit. It took us less than 30minutes to reach our condominium. I went straight away to John's unit, and I was shocked when I entered his unit. It is much better than I have imagined. It is really like what he mentioned. It is windy and has an unblocking mountain view. I was stunted and loss of words at that moment. I started to feel regret for not paying extra for this. If I was considering built to sell the unit, I might have changed my mind to just pay a few thousand extra. John noticed I was amazed at his unit and immediately felt regret on buying city view unit. He began to comfort me. "You know what? The mountain view will be gone soon" he explained. "Look! One project going up at that area, one project over there and one more over there." he continued. "Oh well, the ground works have not started yet, I will foresee you will still have your mountain view for at least 3-4 years," I said. "Yupe, you are absolutely right. My friend was telling me that those two will start to launch next year and that one will start only 2 years later" he continued on his explanation while pointing on the area where those building will be built.

By comparing the pool view and city view unit, although you have to pay a slightly higher price, pool view unit is no doubt a winner over here. This is especially true for properties in Penang Island where the development land is limited. Due to the scarcity of the land, some of the condominiums were built very close to each other. Most of the case, if you bought the city view unit, your view might be blocked, and air circulation might be bad. I wasn't sure how long it took for me to calm down. I became so emotional as this was my first purchased property and I felt like I was conned. After a while, when I regained my control on my mind, I started to digest what he told me just now. I started to feel very curious about how he knew so much about the new developments. I have been following most of the new developments at Penang through developers' website and property blogs, but I didn't notice any news about what he just told me. I started to ask.

"How do you know there will be three developments over there?" I asked. "Good question, I shouldn't have told you so. It is a trade secret from the developer. I guess it is too late now for me to recall now" he laughed. "I have one friend whom I used to be a client to in the past— they're now working with that developer. They acquired that piece of land a year ago. Recently, there is more discussion on what to do with that land. It wasn't that firm yet last month. Now, it is almost finalized." he continued. "What are their plans?" I asked. "Well, I guess my friend is gonna kill me if I continue to tell you more" he hesitated. "Anyway, just keep it within these walls. They plan to build one luxury condo, one middle range condo and then one affordable apartment as repayment for those originally staying at that land. I nodded.

My curiosity did not just stop here. I start to wonder how come he can become friend with a salesperson from the developer. "How can you be so close with a salesperson from the developer? The one I deal with in the past was not that friendly" I questioned. "It is a very long story. I knew him since she was still working as a property agent. I deal with her quite a lot as she always gave me very good deals. Sometimes, I wonder why she didn't grab some of those bargain buys. A few years ago, she left the agency and joined that developer. We kept in touch since I purchased the first unit from her." he explained. There were just too many things to digest from that conversation. It seems like he was investing quite a lot in properties. I always heard that property investment is not always profiting. I wondered what his story is. I probed further.

"You sounded like you invested a lot?" I asked. It seems like his wife overheard what we are discussing. "Yes, he invested too much. That's why he is still driving an old car and staying at middle range condo," she added. I was so shocked. This is only the middle range condo for them? This is the maximum budget I can afford. They don't seem to be old enough to be that rich, and their occupation does not seem to be able to get them that rich too. Out of sudden, his wife continued, "If he lets me stay at his most luxury apartment, I won't be so suffered now." I was completely blanked after I heard that. A moment later, I rephrase my question, "How many properties you hold now?" There is a long pause after this question. It seems like he was doing some computations in his mind. After a while, he replied, "Well, I might have about 15 properties now".

I was getting very excited now. I wanted to know more about this mysterious guy standing in front of me. A guy that is holding 15 properties and live below his means. He looks roughly about 40 years old and holding 15 properties at his age does seem to be mission impossible. I started to forecast his current age. If he graduated at 24 years just like everyone else, if he purchased one property every year, he will probably at 39 years old. "Are you about 39 years old now?" without much hesitation, I asked. Suddenly, his wife chuckled. I knew I said something wrong. "Guess what? I might look older than you thought. I am just about to turn 35." he replied. "I am so so sorry, it is hard for me to imagine that you can hold more than 15 properties at age less than 40," I said. "I don't think there are rules saying you can't" he joked. We burst out laughing.

"I am extremely curious on how you did it? As we are both engineers, we know very clearly that if we solely rely on our monthly salary that is almost impossible, we can achieve what you have now." I explained. "Do you have any side income? Are you from a rich family? Are all your properties which you are holding less than RM100K? Are you joking with me?" I can't stop questioning. "I don't think you expect me to answer everything, right?" he laughed. "Well, yes, I have a side income to help me achieve my goals. My family is doing just okay. My properties are priced between RM135K till RM2.6 Million." he answered. "You haven't answered my last question." I insisted. "Sorry, I missed that. What's that again?" he asked. "Are you joking?" I re-emphasized. "Hey, friend. I start to like you already. Of course not. I am being very serious in every word he promised."

"Do you mind to share more about your success story?" I asked. "Oh boy! Don't ever call it a success. I have

made more mistakes than you can imagine. One thing I did it right is I started at a very young age. How old are you?" he asked. "Well, I am turning 32 this year," I answered. "Okay, so, I bought my first property when I was 29 years old, it was until recently I acquired more than 15 properties. It all happened at last five years," he explained. "You are saying that you acquired 14 properties for the last 5 years," I asked. "You got it right, good maths," he answered. "How did you do it? You won Toto?". His wife chuckled again. "No, no, there is no shortcut, and there is no miracle also. It is done progressively with plenty of hard works" he said. At that point, I don't think the word progressive is the right word to use here.

"You mentioned we need to start early if we want to be successful?" I asked. "That's absolutely correct. The key to success in property investment is to start early. If you come across some articles about housing price, you would notice that housing price typically doubled every 10 years. If you bought 10 years earlier, you would pay 2x cheaper. Why wait?". "Yes, I heard that before. However, that's what everyone is saying, but very few of us turn into action." I said. "Yeap, that's why one action is better than one hundred thoughts or plans," he replied. "I agreed. What do you mean 'progressively done'?" I asked. "It simply means 'dream big, act small'" he answered. "What does it really mean?"

I continue asking. "Hey, you know what? It is getting very late now. Why not you drop by tomorrow and we can continue this topic?" he said. "Ya, come back for the next few days, he won't be able to finish everything within another night. His eyes sparkled whenever he talks about his investment strategy." his wife added. Reluctantly, I said goodbye to John and went back home.The heading style 'Heading 1' can be used from the Quick Styles gallery for the chapter heading.

2. Unravel John's Secret

I was left with thousands of unanswered questions. I have so many to think about and some much to ask. At this point in time, I might not be able to form any question; there are too many information to digest, too many to understand. 14 properties within 5 years, it still sounds impossible. However, when John told me about that, he sounded very confident as if it really happened. The properties price ranged from RM135K to RM2.6 Million. How could that possible? Typical engineer monthly salary is only about RM3K till RM10K. You will need extremely high loan eligibility in order to get a loan for RM2.6 Million property. Will it be his side income that is giving him more cash to perform cash buy? I have a tough time to get asleep that night.

I wasn't able to focus my work also for the next morning. I was telling some of my close friends about John's sharing. None of them were convinced John was telling me the truth. it is totally impossible. Is that really impossible? Or, it is only impossible if you think is impossible. I trusted my instinct, and I believed that John is telling me a real story of himself. It was a long day for me; I was so eager to talk to John again to clear all my doubts. I spent more times looking at my watch than looking at my working documents. Finally, I knocked off sharp at 5pm and went home to unravel John's secret.

I was over excited till I forgot John normally back home about 730pm. I waited impatiently till John reached home at 725pm. I quickly rang John's doorbell and can't wait to continue yesterday topics. "Hey, John!" I greeted. "Hey, Derrick! How are you?" he said. "I am good. Shall we continue?" I asked. "Yes, yes, sure. Can you give me 10mins to take a bath first?" he requested. "Sure!" I answered. Right after that, John went for bathing and left me alone in his living hall. I was glancing around his living hall, and I saw a big bookshelf. I started to analyze what kind of books he normally read. 'Rich dad, poor dad,' 'The intelligent investor,' 'Magic of thinking big,' 'Think and grow rich,' 'Money the master game,' etc. There are more than 100 investment and self-improvement books at his bookshelf. I believe he must have been reading a lot.

"Hey Derrick, sorry to keep you waiting" finally he finished his bathing, and we resumed yesterday discussion. "I saw you have plenty books over there," I said. "Yeap, that's right. I like reading during my leisure time," he answered. "What's your favorite book?" I asked. "Oh, I have few of them. I guess I will choose 'Think Big, Act Small' by Jason Jennings as my favorite." he said. "That's what you told me also yesterday on your property investment strategies, 'think big, act small'" I said. "That's right. Good memory," he replied. "Is that your secret to acquiring 14 properties within 5 years?" I asked. "Absolutely" he nodded.

"What do you mean about think big, act small?" I asked. He took a piece of paper and drawn a picture. "What do you see?"

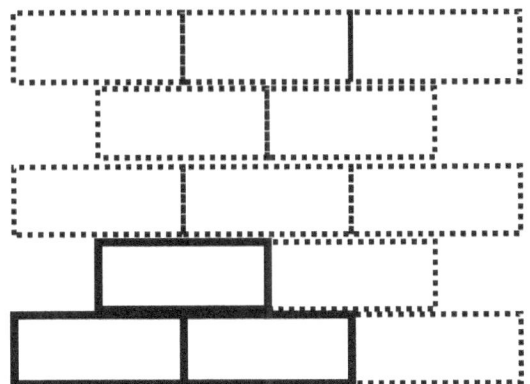

I wasn't sure what he is actually drawing. I was trying hard to link this image with 'think big, act small.' I believe he was trying to explain his theory with this illustration. "It seems like bricks" I answered. "Yes, indeed. Go on!" he encouraged. "It seems like only three of those are placed, the rest are still missing" I continued. "Exactly, oh boy, you have a great imagination. You know what that means? It simply means, if you want to build a wall, you have to lay your bricks one by one. If you want to build a room, you have to build your walls. If you want to build a house, you have to build your rooms." he explained. "I think I get it. You are trying to say; if I want to be successful in property investment, I have to acquire properties one by one." I answered.

"Yes, you got it half right. If you want to build a sustainable wall, you will have to structure it correctly. You will also need to lay them according to the sequence. You have to complete the entire row before you can move on to the next row." he said. "Okay, it is getting deeper now. I can't connect the dots." I said. "Property investment is just like laying bricks. First, you need to develop a plan; then you need to follow through your plan. Do not make any shortcuts or else you will have to restart all over again."

"I start to get it now; can you elaborate more?" I asked. "Sure, I am glad you are catching up. Think big means you will need to have the desire to be successful in property investment. It is a lengthy process, and if you don't have the determination, you will give up very quickly. Act small means you will have to do it step by step. When you get started, it is very easy for you to make a mistake or lose control. If you started with investment which takes up almost all your wealth, it would be very difficult for you to get up again after you failed. No one in this world can predict the property market trend. To be safe, you need to act small. In other words, start with properties which will take a small portion of your wealth. progressively, you move up to the higher end market." he explained.

"Think big, act small is a mindset that governed my investment strategy. At least it is proven successful to me. Once this mindset is wired in your brain, you will have to develop your own plan. For example, if you set to achieve financial freedom through property investment, you will need to calculate how much passive income you need to cover your expenses. Then, you need to calculate how much properties you have to acquire in order to achieve that. You will have to add your deadline also." he continued.

"Sounds interesting. Can you be more precise about setting up your goals and plans?" I asked. "Yeap, but it is very much depending on what you really want. I can give you an example," he answered. He started to draw again on another piece of paper.

Goal	Achieve financial freedom
Time	Within 10 years
Current monthly expenses	RM8K
Extraordinary expenses	RM2K
How?	Generate passive income RM10K
Plan?	Acquire 20 properties which generate cash flow RM500 per month
Specific Plan?	Acquire 2 properties each year which meet the above criteria

"It sounds so simple," I said. "Yeap, it sounds very simple. Typically, you will have a higher success rate if you have simple plans. Fancy or complicated plans normally will only confuse you. However, I have to warn you that not everyone is able to strictly follow the plan." he said. "Most of us can make a simple and effective plan, but not everyone is capable of excelling in property investment. In fact, many property investors were losing money. The main reason is execution. People get extremely emotional when dealing with money. They either too timid to enter the market or too afraid to stay long enough to gain maximum profit." he explained.

"I am sure I won't." I grinned. "I really hope so. Let me ask you one question. Let's say you wish to achieve financial freedom within 10 years and your plan is to acquire 2 properties every year. At the first few years, you are doing fine, and you are doing much better than your target. Your capital appreciation is going higher than expected, and your rental yield is greater than you calculated. Suddenly, the market crashed. Everyone is disposing their stocks, selling their properties and keeping more cash to prepare for rainy days. What will you do?" he asked.

"As you said, I have already achieved good returns for the last few years; I should just cash out and wait for the good timing to enter the market again." I confidently replied. "Well, it seems like you are nothing different compared to the rest. Remember no one in this world can predict when the market will crash and when the market will recover. If KLCI dropped 50 points today, it might increase 70 points tomorrow. In fact, you should do exactly the opposite, when people are disposing in panic, you should quietly acquire them as you will find a lot bargain buys during a downturn. No matter what happens, to be successful in property investment, stick with your game plan." he said.

"So, are you telling me that I need to equip with emotional intelligent in order to be successful in property investment?" I continued to seek clarification. "Derrick, you are learning fast. Exactly. You need to control your emotion in everything you do. It might sound simple, but when it comes to a critical moment, you will be carried away very easily." he emphasized. "Why? I can't imagine I will be carried away." I defended. "Let me give you a scenario. In 2008, when the US property market crash, the property price dropped more than 50%. What will you do?" he asked. "Oh well, like we said, be tough and stay long" I answered. "That's right. It is easier to say when you are not involved in the transaction. Imagine that your property price reduced from 1 Million to 500 thousand, and everyone is disposing their properties, will you follow the flock? I think so." he explained. "And that is exactly we want to avoid" he continued. I finally got his point, no matter what's going on, stick with my own game. Every 10 years, there will be a major market correction and every 3-5 years, there will be a minor market fluctuation.

What we have to do is to ignore all this trend and stay in the plan.

"Your step by step approach sounds very simple, but I don't think it is achievable," I said. "I am glad you noticed some flaws. Tell me what you catch?" he replied. "I don't think you can acquire properties that will generate passive income RM500 per month in Penang." I clarified. "Very good. That's why we need to very different approach in this irrational market. Irrational market simply means that the rental income is not on par with the monthly installment. This normally happens when the property price increased faster than the national income. This is exactly what happened in Penang. For example, I purchased a RM450K property today and apply for a loan with interest of 4.4%; I will be paying roughly about RM2,000 per month. However, the maximum rental income I can get is only about RM1,400 per month. In other words, I am losing RM600 per month." he said. "Absolutely, that doesn't seem like a good investment" I added. "Not really, you forgot about one very important factor. The capital appreciation" he said.

"Capital appreciation? That's not something guaranteed. Should we put in the book? I always heard people saying that don't factor in anything which is not guaranteed" I asked. "If you are talking about guaranteed, then nothing is guaranteed in this world. Rental income is not guaranteed; you will lose it when your tenant steps out. Capital appreciation is not guaranteed; you will lose money when property market crash. Even fixed deposit is not guaranteed, your money and your earned interest will completely wipe out when the bank collapsed. All you need to focus is not what is guaranteed now but what is happening in the last 10 years. The property cycle will probably repeat again for the next 10 years" he said.

"I am getting it now. Can you share me how you alter the plan?" I asked. "Sure, let me draw it out" he replied and at the meantime tearing off another piece of paper from his book.

Goal	Achieve financial freedom
Time	Within 10 years
Current monthly expenses	RM8K
Extraordinary expenses	RM2K
How?	Generate passive income RM10K
Plan?	Acquire sufficient properties which able to generate cash flow RM10,000 per month

Specific Plan?	Acquire 20 properties able to give you more than 2x ROI in 5 years. Dispose 10 properties which market value increased more than double in the 10th year. Pay off more than 50% debt for remaining properties on hand with the capital gain Enjoy your positive cash flow.

"You are bringing this investment plan into a new level now. I am not sure I still follow." I said. "It will be a very long discussion if we want to dive in Return on Investment topic. I will propose we do it another day. I believe it is more than enough for you to digest today." he said. "Right." I chuckled. "Since we are talking about investment plan, there are few more things I would like you to suggest to you also. Is your company practicing PDCA methodology?" he asked. "Yeah, Plan Do Check Act is very common in most of the engineering company," I answered. "Use that as your tool in property investment," he said. "PDCA?" I unbelievably asked. "Yes, PDCA. Here are the golden rules" he said.

Plan	Understand your objectives, set your goals and targets Plan ahead, don't rush in
Do	Follow your plan, don't get emotional Don't hesitate; good deals go fast
Check	Keep track on your income and expenses Make sure to meet your ROI target
Act	Revise your plan if necessary, but any revision must not deviate from your objectives, goals, and targets

"Make sense?" he asked. "Certainly," I answered. I was overwhelmed with so many new ideas, and I can no longer digest what John was telling me anymore. John noticed that too, and he suggested that we can cover other topics another day.

3. Return on Investment

Although I am working in engineering film, my math was terrible. We spent more than 5 nights together just to understand the return on investment concept. John has been a very good teacher and kind enough to share me what he knows and what he thinks we should do to be successful.

Return on investment or ROI simply means how much you invested and how much you received as returns in later date. For example, I invested RM100, and I received RM200 in returns after 5 years. My ROI is 2x in 5 years.

Invest	RM100
Return	RM200
ROI	2x

This concept is very easy to understand, but it will be a lot difficult when we use this similar concept with property investment. John laid it down one by one for me to understand, just like what he mentioned earlier that property investment is just like laying bricks. ROI can further breakdown into income and expenses.

Invest	Expenses
Return	Income - Expenses
ROI	(Income - Expenses) / Expenses

Next, he walked me through what is considered as income and expenses in property investment. Most of them are already very familiar to most of us. Nevertheless, we should take a look again on them to ensure we really understand them. It is extremely important for us to understand them before we can calculate ROI correctly. It is very risky to develop plans or targets with wrong ROI computation.

Income	1. Capital Appreciation 2. Rental Income
Expenses	1. Down payment 2. Agent Fees (Buy and Rent) 3. Stamp Duty 4. Legal Fees 5. Maintenance Fees and Sinking Fund 6. Quit Rent 7. Assessment Fees 8. Repairing Fees 9. Renovation and Furnishing Fees 10. Mortgage Interest

Next, John helped us to tackle those listed items one by one. Reasonably, he was calculating the ROI in 5 years time frame. He mentioned any properties which is able to give you ROI 2x within 5 years is good to acquire.

Capital Appreciation

When he calculated the potential capital appreciation, he looks at the big picture. He did not focus only on property price in recent months or recent years. He looked back to the housing market performance for the last 10 years and conservatively estimated the potential uprise of the property price.

In every 10 years, the property price will increase more than double. In other words, the property which you acquire today at market value, it's property price will double in 10 years later. That is equivalent to a 7% increase in yearly basis. Assuming property price increases 7% per year, the property value will increase by 197% after 10 years.

Property value $= 1.07^{10}$ x property price

$= 197\%$ property price

Rental Income

Apart from capital appreciation, rental income is another item which is difficult to estimate. Rental income differs significantly due to property type, location, occupancy rate, security, facilities, etc. In order to have stabilize rental income, John said that you have to develop a diversified portfolio. In other words, you have to acquire lower end, higher end, and middle range property. Your portfolio will have to consists of different property type to serve different market needs. In general, in calculating rental income, John conservatively uses 3% rental yield. Rental yield is simply the annual rental income divided by property purchase price. It is actually a lot lower than a developed country like Singapore or Hong Kong. However, 3-4% rental yield is what we are experiencing in average in Penang market now.

In overall, lower end property will normally give you higher yielding as there is more demand. Nevertheless, the tenant quality is poorer as they have lower household income and their monthly payment might be inconsistent. Take an example on RM400K property, 3% rental yield will give you RM1,000 rental income per month. Nevertheless, the actual rental yield is even lower as you have to still have to pay maintenance fees, quit rent and assessment fees.

	Low-End Property	Middle Range Property	High-End Property
Property Name	Jalan Tengah Flat	Sunnyville	By The Sea
Property Price	RM135,000	RM400,000	RM1,400,000
Location	Bayan Lepas	Bayan Baru	Batu Ferringhi
Monthly Rental	RM650	RM1,300	RM3,500
Annual Rental	RM7,800	RM15,600	RM42,000
Rental Yield	5.80%	3.90%	3.00%

Down payment

Down Payment is something we paid upfront to acquire a property. It is typically 10% of the property purchase price. For example, if we want to acquire RM400K property, we have to pay 40K down payment and the remaining 90% or RM360K we can apply loan. Meanwhile, if you have more than 2 residential property with loan, you have to pay 30% down payment and apply 70% loan. Nevertheless, there are multiple ways to reduce down payment. To be successful, as a property investor, you need to creatively reduce your down payment. You will only be able to acquire more properties if you are able to hold more cash on hand. To keep more cash on hand, it will be a lot easier to spend them wisely than to accumulate again from zero.

Ways to reduce down payment-

1. Buy new development where developers provide significant down payment rebate
2. Negotiate with the seller to provide down payment rebate
3. Negotiate with the seller to repay the down payment through few installments
4. Buy under market value property and refinance the property to cash back the down payment paid

It is not advisable to go buy new development as that will lock down your loan eligibility. Healthy cash flow and high loan eligibility are two key points to acquire properties continuously. If you purchase a new 400K property which will only complete after 4 years, your loan eligibility is locked for 4 years, and you won't be able to generate rental income and regain your loan eligibility. Your investment plan will be delayed. John reminded us that time is our biggest enemy in property investment.

The preferable option is to get down payment rebate from sellers. If you have good negotiation skills, you will be able to convince sellers to give you up to 30% down payment rebate. This is extremely crucial when you have already acquired more than 2 units with a loan.

Agent Fees

Agent fees are a commission that we paid to property agents as a return on the services provided. Services include renting out and selling off the unit. In Penang, agent fees are normally is 1% of property selling price and 1 month rental for 1 year tenancy contract.

For example:

Property selling price RM400K: Agent fees- RM4K

Property monthly rental RM1K, Agent fees- RM1K

John mentioned that some of us would argue to save cost by selling off or renting out without going through a property agent. However, he strongly advised us to engage with good and trustworthy property agent. He emphasized that if you have a good runner, it will save you a lot of hassles. It makes sense to use DIY (Do It Yourselves) method if you are dealing only for 1-2 properties. If you are dealing with 5-10 properties, you won't be able to do it all by yourselves. Furthermore, experienced property agents have large network which is able to sell off or rent out your properties with a much better price. Let the expert take care of your assets. Delegating is the only way to go farther.

Legal Fees and Stamp Duty

Legal fees and stamp duty are payable when you acquire new property. Those fees are higher when your property acquisition price is higher. You will have to pay legal fees and stamp duty for both SPA (Sales and Purchase Agreement) and LA (Loan Agreement). In details, John shared the calculations for legal fees and stamp duty.

Legal Fees for both SPA and LA

Legal Fees Tier	Tiered Rate
First 500,000	1.00%
Next 500,000	0.80%
Next 2,000,000	0.70%

Next 2,000,000	0.60%
Thereafter	0.50%

Stamp duty for SPA

Legal Fees Tier	Tiered Rate
First 500,000	1.00%
Next 500,000	0.80%
Next 2,000,000	0.70%
Next 2,000,000	0.60%
Thereafter	0.50%

Stamp duty for LA

Stamp Duty Tier	Tiered Rate
Any amount	0.50%

John noticed that I was very confused about the Tiered rate and he gave one example to better understanding the computation. He was using RM800K property for example-

Down payment: RM80K

Loan amount: RM720K

SPA- Legal Fees and Stamp Duty

Legal Fees Tier	Tiered Price	Tiered Rate	Payable
First 500,000	500,000	1.00%	5,000
Next 500,000	300,000	0.80%	2,400
Next 2,000,000		0.70%	
Next 2,000,000		0.60%	
Thereafter		0.50%	
	Total Payable		7,400

Stamp Duty Tier	Tiered Price	Tiered Rate	Payable
First 100,000	100,000	1.00%	1,000
Next 400,000	400,000	2.00%	8,000
Thereafter	300,000	3.00%	9,000

LA- Legal Fees and Stamp Duty

Legal Fees Tier	Tiered Price	Tiered Rate	Payable
First 500,000	500,000	1.00%	5,000
Next 500,000	220,000	0.80%	1,760

Next 2,000,000		0.70%	
Next 2,000,000		0.60%	
Thereafter		0.50%	
	Total Payable		6,760

Stamp Duty Tier	Tiered Price	Tiered Rate	Payable
Any amount	720,000	0.50%	3,600
	Total Payable		3,600

Total payable-

SPA	Payable
Legal Fees	7,400
Stamp Duty	18,000
LA	
Legal Fees	6,760
Stamp Duty	3,600
Total Payable	35,760

Maintenance Fees and Sinking Fund

Maintenance fees and sinking fund is normally paid to apartment or condominium management office to manage or maintain the entire building including facilities. Typically, higher end property will incur higher maintenance fees. However, if you calculate the maintenance fees using property price as the denominator, you will interestingly find that the maintenance fees are about 0.6% of the property price. However, this assumption is only valid for an apartment, condominium or gated and guarded landed properties. In ROI calculation, John is using this 0.6% assumption.

	Low-End Property	Middle Range Property	High-End Property
Property Name	Jalan Tengah Flat	Sunnyville Condo	By The Sea Condo
Property Price	RM135K	RM400K	RM1,400K
Location	Bayan Lepas	Bayan Baru	Batu Ferringhi
Maintenance Fees + Sinking Fund	RM55	RM195	RM795
	0.50%	0.60%	0.70%

Quit Rent and Assessment Fees

Quit Rent and Assessment Fees are very different for different property type and property title. For example, the commercial title is normally about 2 times higher than the residential title. In average, for residential title property, the assessment fees and quit rent is about 0.15% of the property price.

	Low-End Property	Middle Range Property	High-End Property
Property Name	Jalan Tengah Flat	Sunnyville Condo	By The Sea Condo
Property Price	RM135K	RM400K	RM1,400K
Location	Bayan Lepas	Bayan Baru	Batu Ferringhi
Assessment Fees	RM200	RM577	RM1,200
Quit Rent	RM6	RM12	RM84
	0.15%	0.15%	0.09%

Property renovation, furnishing and repairing cost

Typically, you will need to spend about RM15K-40K to renovate and furnish your newly purchased unit. Nevertheless, if you are able to buy a fully renovated and furnished unit, you will save a lot of cash. John advised us that never rent out empty unit because it takes months to successfully rent out and the rental income will significantly impact. However, it is not wise to buy a fully renovated and furnished unit if those units are selling much higher than market value. Sometimes, it makes more sense to buy the original unit, renovate and rent out while sometimes, it makes sense to buy fully renovated and furnished unit and rent out directly. John said that we have to be very flexible on this, but we have to make sure the ROI is 2x within 5 years. Renovation, furnishing and repairing cost is about RM15K for a low-end property, RM25K for middle range property and RM40K for high-end property.

	Low-End Property	Middle Range Property	High-End Property
Property Name	Jalan Tengah Flat	Sunnyville Condo	By The Sea Condo
Property Price	RM135K	RM400K	RM1,400K
Location	Bayan Lepas	Bayan Baru	Batu Ferringhi
Renovation Fees	RM8,000	RM15,000	RM25,000
Furnishing Fees	RM5,000	RM8,000	RM15,000
Total	RM13,000	RM23,000	RM40,000

Mortgage Interest

Mortgage interest is normally very difficult to estimate, but John makes it feel very easy. Loan interest rate is typically lower for a high-end property as the loan amount is larger. Based on John's experience, interest rate is normally 0.2% lower for loan amount more than RM1 Million while the interest rate is typically 0.2% higher for a loan amount less than RM200K. In general, for loan tenure of 30 years, mortgage interest paid within 5 years is typically 19% of your property purchase price.

	Low-End Property	Middle Range Property	High-End Property
Property Name	Jalan Tengah Flat	Sunnyville Condo	By The Sea Condo
Property Price	RM135K	RM400K	RM1,400K
Location	Bayan Lepas	Bayan Baru	Batu Ferringhi
Loan Amount	RM121.5K	RM360K	RM1,260K
Loan Period	30	30	30
Interest Rate	4.60%	4.45%	4.20%
Mortgage Interest in 5years	RM26,795	RM76,722	RM252,976

	19.85%	19.18%	18.07%

Finally, John had covered all the important items which required to calculate ROI. At the end of the discussion, after more than 5 nights discussion, he emphasized that the rules of thumb are to acquire property which is capable of providing 2 times ROI within 5 years. He then helped me to recap what he had taught me.

	Item	Assumption
Income	Capital Appreciation	Annual increment: 7%
	Rental Income	Rental Yield: 3%
Expenses	Down payment	10% of the purchase price
	Agent Fees	Buy: 1% of the selling price Rent: 1 month for 1 year tenancy contract
	Legal Fees and Stamp Duty	Use Tiered rate provided
	Maintenance Fees and Sinking Fund	0.6% of the property price
	Quit Rent and Assessment Fees	0.15% of property price

	Renovation and Furnishing Fees	Low-end property: RM15K Middle range property: RM25K High-end property: RM45K
	Mortgage Interests in 5 years (30 years loan tenure)	19.0% of the property price

4. Acquiring 10 Properties Within 5 Years

I have been spending most of my nights with John for the last few weeks. To be honest, I learned a lot from John. However, when I start to digest the information I have gathered so far, I found out that I still don't have much idea on acquiring 10 properties within 5 years. I figured out I have to ask John directly at next meet up.

On the next day, I went to John's unit again. "Hey, John!" I greeted. "Hey, Derrick! Come in please" he replied. "I believe you have already digested all the information and provided and you want to get down to business now" he continued. I was very surprised that he knew my hidden agenda. I guess I can directly clarify my doubts. "Thanks for coaching me on the ROI calculation, those are very good learning; however, I would like to know how to acquire 10 properties within 5 years," I said.

"I knew you would have many questions after you digest all the information I gave a few days back. However, I am still a little disappointed with your question. It seems like you haven't recognized the rules I have been telling you. Remember when I told you about defining your objective, your plan, and your target. It is not how much you buy within 5 years; it is how much you need to buy within 5 years. Have you done your calculation? You might need to buy more properties than me if your monthly expenses are greater than me." he said.

"Well, you are right. I will have to do my own maths first before I can decide how much I need to buy within 5 years" I said. "Let me rephrase my question, how can I acquire properties in faster rate?" I asked. "That's a more relevant question" he grinned. In general, there are few rules of thumb which I actually told you before in the last few discussions.

How to acquire properties in faster rate?

Rule1: Acquire only properties with 2 times return on investment within 5 years

Rule2: Do not let go of cash and loan eligibility easily. Make sure you gain it back if you let it go

Rule3: Delegating your tasks

"Well, we have been discussing about ROI for last few nights. I guess now it is time to let you know how to increase your ROI for all property you acquire. There are few items that will greatly increase your ROI if you know the tricks" he explained.

Action	Normal	Improved
Higher rental income with a fully renovated and furnished unit	3.00%	4.00%
Negotiate with the seller to reduce down payment	10.00%	0.00%
Engage with only a few agents to get discounts at property agent fees	None	Up to 50% discount
Engage with only a few lawyers to get discounts at legal fees	None	Up to 50% discount
Engage with only a few contractors to get discounts at renovation and furnishing fees	None	20% discount
Engage with only a few bankers to get a better interest rate	None	0.1% better

"Interesting. I was wondering how much ROI will improve if I did all those actions that you just listed down" I replied. "Let's do some calculation then," he suggested.

ROI within 5 years

Property price: RM400K

Normal interest rate: 4.45%

Loan tenure: 30 years

Item	Normal	Improved
Capital Appreciation	RM161K (7%)	RM161K (7%)
Rental Income	RM60K (3.0%)	RM80K (4.0%)
Income in 5 years	RM221,000	RM241,000
Down payment	40K (10.0%)	RM0 (0.0%)
Agent Fees	Buy: RM4K Rent: RM5K (5years)	Buy: RM2K Rent: RM2.5K (5years)
Legal Fees and Stamp Duty	Stamp duty: RM9K Legal Fees: RM8K	Stamp duty: RM9K Legal Fees: RM4K
Maintenance Fees and Sinking Fund	RM12K (5 years)	RM12K (5 years)
Quit Rent and Assessment Fees	RM3K (5 years)	RM3K (5 years)
Renovation and Furnishing Fees	RM25K	RM20K
Mortgage Interests in 5 years	RM76,722 (5 years, RM360K, 4.45%)	RM83,271 (5 years, RM400K, 4.35%)

| Expenses in 5 years | RM179,722 | RM135,771 |
| ROI in 5 years | 1.23x | 1.78x |

"Wow, that was amazing. The ROI in 5 years just increase from 1.23x to 1.78x." I commented. "Yeah, that's right. If you break it down to interest rate per year, it is about 12% for the improved scenario versus roughly 4% for the normal scenario." he further explained. "If that's the case why do I want to invest in properties if the return is almost the same as the fixed deposit?" I asked. "You got the point. If you are not good at playing this investment game, you better put your money in a fixed deposit. similar gain with lower risk." he nodded. "Ready to do math for 10 years?" he asked. "Yeah, can't wait" I excitedly said.

ROI within 10 years

Property price: RM400K

Normal interest rate: 4.45%

Loan tenure: 30 years

Item	Normal	Improved
Capital Appreciation	RM387K (7%)	RM387K (7%)

Rental Income	RM120K (3.0%)	RM160K (4.0%)
Income in 10 years	RM507,000	RM547,000
Down payment	40K (10.0%)	RM0 (0.0%)
Agent Fees	Buy: RM4K Rent: RM10K (10years)	Buy: RM2K Rent: RM5K (10years)
Legal Fees and Stamp Duty	Stamp duty: RM9K Legal Fees: RM8K	Stamp duty: RM9K Legal Fees: RM4K
Maintenance Fees and Sinking Fund	RM24K (10 years)	RM24K (10 years)
Quit Rent and Assessment Fees	RM6K (10 years)	RM6K (10 years)
Renovation and Furnishing Fees	RM35K	RM28K
Mortgage Interests in 10 years	RM145,467 (10years, RM360K, 4.45%)	RM157,762 (10years, RM400K, 4.35%)
Expenses in 10 years	RM281,567	RM235,762
ROI in 10 years	1.8x	2.32x

"Fantastic. The improved scenario is yielding whopping 2.32x within 10 years." I shouted. "Yes, it is very attractive numbers, bear in mind that this is still very conservative calculation. In fact, most of my properties are doing much better than this numbers" he explained. "Oh mine, how much ROI in 5 years that your current holding is giving you?" I asked curiously. "It is average 2.0x ROI in 5 years," he said. "Are you ready to learn about the second rule now?" he asked. "Yes, yes, I am getting super excited now" I was over-excited at that moment. It feels like I will become a millionaire very soon if I follow his path.

"What's the second rule?" he asked. I was too excited that I have to refer to my notes to recall the second rule.

Rule 2: Do not let go of cash and loan eligibility easily. Make sure you gain it back if you let it go

"Why is cash and loan eligibility so important?" he asked. "I believe this is the key criteria to buy more properties" I answered confidently. "That's right. How do you keep more cash?" he asked again. "Well, few options. I can reduce down payment, reduce agent fees, legal fees, decrease renovation and furnishing cost" I replied. "That's correct. You are getting the point. How do you ensure you don't lose loan eligibility?" he asked. "I guess I buy everything by cash?" I answered. "Yes, that's correct, but it is unwise to do so. If you purchase without a loan, you won't be able to purchase property in faster rate" he explained. "As an engineer, we both know that the biggest challenge we have is to accumulate cash. Thanks to our consistent low income" he said. "Totally agreed" I laughed. "How do you maintain loan eligibility and cash altogether?" I asked.

"The only possible way is BRDB" he explained. "BRDB?" I was confused. "Buy-Rent-Declare-Buy," he said. "What does that mean? Can you shed some lights?" I was a little bit losing my patient as I eagerly want to know more about it. "There are few guidelines to be successful in BRDB. It is very simple plan, but it is difficult to follow" he said.

		Guidelines
B	Buy	Buy with a minimum down payment (Zero down payment)
R	Rent	Rent with maximum rental yield (>4% rental yield)
D	Declare	Declare rental income to regain loan eligibility

B	Buy	Buy with a minimum down payment (Zero down payment)

"You should know how to buy with minimum down payment and to maximize rental income by now. Do you how to declare rental income?" he asked. "I guess I will just share my tenancy agreement to the banker and banker should be able to recognize my rental income" I answered. "Well, you are partially right. Anyway, good try. For banks to recognize your rental income, you will need to have stamped tenancy agreement and bank statement which clearly shows rental crediting" he said. "I see. It is not that straight forward then" I grinned.

"Before you acquire housing loan, you will have to calculate estimated loan payment and potential rental income. Your goal is to maximize your rental income and minimize your loan payment in order to maintain your loan eligibility. In Penang, it is very difficult to acquire property which can fully pay off your monthly installment. Nevertheless, 5 years later, you will have a higher chance that your rental income will exceed your monthly installment" he said. He also showed me an example to prove his concept.

N-park apartment, Bayan Baru, Penang

	2008	2018
Selling Price	RM170K	RM350K
Loan amount	RM153K	RM315K
Loan interest rate	4.45%	4.45%
Loan tenure	30 years	30 years
Monthly instalment	RM770	RM1,587
Monthly rental	RM600	RM1,000

From the example provided by John, you can clearly see that if you acquired the said property in 2008, your rental income would be higher than your monthly installment in 2018. However, you will look back to the monthly rental when you bought your unit at 2008; your rental income is still unable to fully cover your monthly installment. In order words, it will be difficult to have rental income fully cover the monthly installment for the first few years after you acquire your new property. John also emphasized that the longer you hold on your property, the higher the passive income you can expect.

"Alright, I got it now. Both the first and second rules make sense to me now. How about the third rule? What do you mean about delegating your task? Is it similar to what my boss delegate works to me?" I asked. "Exactly, the only difference now is that you will have to delegate your tasks instead of given assigned task. Sometimes, it is a lot easier to execute on assigned task than to delegate tasks to others. There are a couple of skills that you have to acquire before you can delegate your tasks successfully to others" he said. "I never thought delegating is difficult, I guess my boss makes it feel very easy then" I laughed. "To successfully delegate tasks, you will need to have good communication skills as you have to clearly state what you want them to do. Besides, you will have to perform multiple screening until you found someone whom you can trust. Finally, you will need to have the characteristic that will motivate them to work for you" he said.

Delegating golden rules

1. Clearly, state what you want to achieve

2. Find someone whom you can trust and trusted you

3. Motivate your followers to work for you

"In property investment, it is impossible to handle all the properties all by yourselves if you have more than 5 properties. Even handling 2-3 properties are extremely tiring. Imagine the tasks you have to tackle all by yourselves if you want to do it all by yourselves" he added. Then, he started to list all the tiring and troublesome tasks to tackle if you handle all by yourselves.

DIY Tasks

1. Arrange an appointment with multiple property owners for property viewing

2. Handle the earnest deposit by your own. You might even be conned as some of the claimed owners might not be the real owner

3. Submit your earnest deposit to the lawyer

4. Submit your earnest deposit to bankers

5. Look for bankers' contact for loan application

6. Filter the banker who provides the best interest rate

7. Renovate and furnish your unit by yourselves

The list will go even longer if I didn't stop John. "Hey John, I got it, it makes more sense to leave it to the experts" I knew John is testing my patience level. "I am wondering when you will ask me to stop" he laughed. "You have to define professionals whom you can trust. Once you found someone trustworthy and after they trusted you, you can start to delegate your task. You need to engage with property agents to buy new units or to rent out your existing units. You need to engage with lawyers to provide you legal services such as title transfer, sales and purchase agreement signing, loan agreement signing, tenancy agreement signing, etc. You need to engage banker for bank loan application and refinancing if needed. Finally, you need to engage a contractor who can help you to renovate your new unit" he explained. "It seems like I have to build the whole team to support my property investment" I was shocked.

"Yes, you certainly need to build a strong team to be successful" he added. "Do you still remember when we discuss the ROI, we put down two scenarios; normal scenario and improved scenario? If you put more focus on that draft carefully, you will notice that your expenses will reduce if you have an engaged team" he explained while highlighting those reduced expenses due to professionals that you engaged.

Action	Normal	Improved
Higher rental income with a fully renovated and furnished unit	3.00%	4.00%
Negotiate with the seller to reduce down payment	10.00%	0.00%
Engage with only a few agents to get discounts at property agent fees	None	Up to 50% discount
Engage with only a few lawyers to get discounts at legal fees	None	50% discount
Engage with only a few contractors to get discounts at renovation and furnishing fees	None	20% discount
Engage with only a few bankers to get a better interest rate	None	0.1% better

"So, the two benefits of delegating your property investment tasks are to get better discounts and free up your time?" I asked. "Brilliant, absolutely. You will have more time for property hunting if you free up your time. As I mentioned multiple times, time is your biggest enemy. Don't get defeated by the time" he said.

Benefits of delegating to your engaged agents:

1. Reduce your fees
2. Free up your time

Before I went to sleep that night, I relook into the notes I made just now during our discussion to ensure that guidance wired into my brain. There are many suggestions and advice given by John. Nevertheless, the most important guidance for me is the three rules to acquire properties at a faster pace.

How to acquire properties in faster rate?

Rule1: Acquire only properties with 2 times return on investment within 5 years

Rule2: Do not let go of cash and loan eligibility easily. Make sure you gain it back if you let it go

Rule3: Delegating your tasks

5. Biggest Mistake: Buy And Stay

One day, after dinner together with John, we have another chit-chat session. "Hey John, how long have you been investing in the property market?" I asked. "It has been almost 8 years. I started when I came back from Singapore 8 years ago" he answered. "No wonder you can acquire so many properties. I believe this is because of your savings while you are working in Singapore" I said. "Nope, that's not true; all I have saved is the amount of money which is sufficient to pay the down payment for the first property. If I was working in Malaysia, I believe if I spent wisely, I would have saved that amount of money also" he clarified. "So, what happened? Why won't you make any significant savings while you were in Singapore?" I asked. "That is because I visited Marina Bay Sand too frequent. Luckily Penang is far away from Genting Highlands, and my gambling desire is not strong enough till I willing to travel all the way down to Genting" he laughed.

"I am glad you put your focus in property investment now. It sure gets you more returns than gambling" I said. "Yes, agreed, my wife is the happiest people after I quit gambling," he said. "Did you make any mistakes in the past during property investment?" I asked. "I sure did, in fact, I frequently made wrong judgment calls until today. Although the frequency is much lower now, I do make mistakes occasionally" he said. "I can't imagine. Can you share some of your mistakes?" I asked. "Let me see" he hesitated. "Let me share you one of my biggest mistake which is more relevant to your current state," he said. "Oh great, come on, I am listening" I replied.

"The biggest mistake I made was the very first property I bought back in 2009 when I returned to Penang from Singapore. I was so eager to get my own condominium that I made an emotional decision. I purchased one nicely renovated and furnished Sunnyville unit with a purchase price of RM410K. I paid 10% down payment and paid off all the agent fees, legal fees, and stamp duty. I successfully obtained a 90% loan with an interest rate of 4.2% and 40 years of loan tenure. Two months later, I got my keys after bank loan release. Once I received the keys, I bought some necessities and moved into the condominium with my wife happily. As the unit was in move-in condition, I didn't spend much in renovation and furnishing" he said. "Okay, sounds good. Can you tell me what's happened after that?" I asked I am actually expecting something bad happened after that.

"What do you mean?" he asked. "I didn't hear anything bad yet; I thought that something might have happened after what you just mentioned. For example, the water pipe is not working well because it is an old apartment, electric trip too frequent, or something else which is really bad" I said. "No, no, I have already mentioned all the bad things; you were not paying attention," he said. I was shocked as everything seems pretty normal to me. At the next few hours, John is actually breaking down his mistakes one by one from that property acquisition.

Purchase price of RM410K

John told me that he was very emotional during that time as he always has a target to acquire one property before he turns 28 years old. He did not survey enough, and he made his decision within 2 days after viewing only 2 apartments. Although that unit was fully renovated and furnished, it was already 20 years old when he bought that property. Capital appreciation of that unit is very low because there are fewer demands for old units as they're prone to have more issue. For example, wall starts to crack; electric supply become unstable, water piping is not robust, air-condition piping is leaky, water leak from walls and ceiling, main water storage is dirty and leaky, etc. In fact, you will have to spend more money to restore the unit.

For the interior, you are still able to renovate to improve the condition of the unit. However, for the exterior, it is very difficult. That is because, for old property, many people are unwilling to pay their maintenance fees. Most of the units were sitting idle, and no one is actually staying there. Due to that, Condo management team will have an insufficient fund to maintain the unit probably. The damaged gym facilities might not be able to replace; the swimming pool was left unmanaged with algae, the road to car parks was bumpy, the wall painting is old and dirty, the lift was frequently malfunction, the food at the cafeteria was terrible and poorly managed, etc.

Apart from that, John mentioned another mistake that he made was he didn't inspect the unit probably. He was amazed at the modern renovation and furnishing. The unit was painted with bright color, the floor was laminated with wood alike material, plaster ceiling was probably done with warm downlight, built in wardrobe was beautifully done, enclosed kitchen with all new kitchen cabinet, wall mounted 60-inch LED TV at master bedroom, proper partition at both the master bedroom bathroom and common bathroom, etc.

He was so amazed till he forgot to pay attention to something extremely important, the ceiling. At the common bathroom, there is serious water leaking problem from the unit above that causes the plaster ceiling to have huge watermark. This is very crucial, especially for an apartment or condo. By law, property owner for unit above should fix their leaking problem. However, you will have to negotiate or even argue to get things done. At the end of the day, you might be paying the bill to fix all the bathroom tiles for the unit above. John urged us to look up before you make a deposit.

At that point in time, Sunnyville market value was only about RM380K. John was naive enough to think that the RM410K is reasonable due to the extra renovation and furnishing given. However, as soon as he moved in, he found that some of the renovation and furnishing does not really fit him and he will have to spend some money to fix them. For example, the hanging wardrobe at master bedroom was too small, although it is fancy to look at, but not practical; the partition at bathroom looks practical but when you bath, the water will trap inside the partition as the draining pipe was situated outside the partition, etc.

John reminded us that never significantly overpay any property because of the fancy renovation or furnishing. If you are looking for a renovated unit, make sure it is practical and not too costly to acquire. You would need to do some homework to see how much others were selling before you make your offering. Make it a habit that always ask for RM10K-RM20K lower than market value.

Down payment of RM41K

John mentioned that he brought RM70K-80K cash from Singapore after working there for almost 3 years. He decided to use that money wisely to buy a used car and a property. He spent RM10K for a car down payment for an 8 years old Honda City, and he spent almost RM70K when he purchased Sunnyville unit. He was paying RM41K down payment and about RM25K for other expenses such as legal fees, agent fees, and stamp duty. His savings from 2 years working in Singapore was completely wiped off within that month. He was shocked and feeling very uncomfortable because he doesn't have much cash reserve for rainy days. If something happens during that time, he will be deeply in trouble.

That time, he also wondered whether he had any alternative. Will it be always so tough to acquire new property? He didn't have someone like himself to guide him. That's where he started to study himself, doing a survey and trying to follow the path of the successful property investor. As also mentioned in the previous chapter, always negotiate to minimize down payment. Cash and loan eligibility are key tools for you to acquire more properties.

Loan interest rate of 4.2%

When John acquires Sunnyville, the nominal loan interest rate is 4.2%. He thought that he was offered a nominal loan interest rate and he did not have any second thoughts on it. He accepted the loan interest rate and signed the loan offer letter. In fact, he should have challenged on the rate, as that is his first unit and he has a good basic salary and pays master, he should be getting a lower loan interest rate. Loan interest rate normally differs on your financial scores. Your outstanding debts; monthly payment at credit card bills; education loans; housing loans and car loans; your savings; your net worth will define your scores.

At that moment, John has RM80K savings, basic salary of RM6K, no outstanding debts, a good record at credit card payment and RM40K-50K worth of stocks. If he questions the interest rate or he compares the interest rate from multiple banks, he might have gotten a lower interest rate deal. 0.1% or 0.2% interest rate difference will differ a lot in longer horizon. John also showed us the numbers in order for us to better appreciate what he meant.

Selling Price	RM1 Million	RM1 Million	RM1 Million
Loan amount	RM900K	RM900K	RM900K
Loan interest rate	4.20%	4.10%	4.00%
Loan tenure	30 years	30 years	30 years
Total Interest pay	RM685K	RM665K	RM647K

He emphasized that if you are getting RM900K loan, 4.2% and 4.0% will make you paying RM38K interest in extra. You should always negotiate and compare the loan interest rate to prevent paying extra.

Loan tenure of 40 years

When John noticed that most of his savings were wiped out from paying down payment, agent fees, legal fees, and stamp duty, he was very worried that he won't be able to pay off the monthly installment as doesn't have any backup fund if anything happens. His banker suggested him to get loan tenure of 40 years to lower down the monthly installment. He doesn't know that his banker is not helping him; he is actually trying to earn more interest from his loan.

At that time, John had limited financial knowledge; he accepted the suggestion from his banker. That decision caused him to pay a lot more interest that he supposed to be. Again, he drew out the comparison to let us understand better.

Selling Price	RM1 Million	RM1 Million	RM1 Million
Loan amount	RM900K	RM900K	RM900K
Loan interest rate	4.20%	4.20%	4.20%
Loan tenure	40 years	30 years	20 years

Total Interest payable	RM960K	RM684K	RM432K
Monthly Instalment	RM3.9K	RM4.4K	RM5.5K

Based on the sketch from John, you can clearly observe that the total interest payable differs a lot when you have different loan tenure. The interest payable for 20 years loan tenure is almost 2 times lower than 40 years loan tenure. However, John reminded us that we need not be too aggressive in minimizing the total interest payable. If you lower down your loan tenure too aggressively, you will end up with higher monthly installment which will also consume your loan eligibility. Looking into the numbers from the sketch, the best option is 30 years tenure as the monthly installment is reasonable (only RM500 different from 40 years loan tenure) and the total interest payable is RM276K lower. John reminded us that different loan interest rate, loan amount, expected rental income and other factors might alter your decision on selecting the best loan tenure. What you have to do is to lay down all the numbers and look for the best option. 30 years might not be the best loan tenure for all scenario.

The worst of all, buy and stay strategy

I was very surprised at the fifth mistake that John stated. I thought it would be perfectly fine to buy and stay at your own property. It always seems to be wise to buy ourselves instead of paying rent to others. However, John has a very different view on this. "I was very surprised on the fifth item," I said. "I will be very surprised if you are not" John replied. "If that's so, why do you put this as a mistake?" I asked. A little angry because that is exactly what I am doing now. I am not sure what John is thinking. Should I go ahead and rent out my beloved unit now? No way. "Nope, I did it absolutely right to list it here. In fact, this is the biggest mistake of all time" he said. "Tell me more" I was starting to lose my patience. "Few things will happen if you buy and stay for your first property. That is the main reason why everyone stuck in the rat race. If you are doing this at a very young age, probably 30 years old or below, you will find out that you won't be able to be successful in property investment" he explained. "I still don't get it" I argued. "Don't get mad first, let me walk you through on this. Keep an open mind please," he said patiently.

"When you bought your very first property, you might be broke because you almost spent all your money during your property acquisition and you consumed more than 50% of your loan eligibility. You won't be able to hunt down another property because you don't have cash and loan eligibility now," he explained. I nodded as a sign of agreement. "You might argue that eventually, you will save enough for a down payment for another unit and your paycheck will improve, and hence your loan eligibility will improve. However, in reality, after few years of working, you will notice that big portion of your money was used to pay off the housing and car loans and you are still broke after few years" he continued. "There are multiple reasons for this, most common reasons are getting married, giving birth, need a larger apartment for own stay, need to get a larger car, etc.," he said.

"So, that's why you said you would trap in rat race" finally I started to appreciate his points. "Absolutely" he laughed. "I thought you mentioned you bought your very first unit is for own stay too. How do you overcome or get out of the rat race?" I asked. "I knew that question would come. After 1-2 years of staying at my apartment, I realized that my bank account still fluctuates between RM10K to RM20K only. And, it doesn't seem like it will improve in the next few years. I knew something needed to change, and I knew clearly it has to be done immediately" he said.

"The next day, I shared my plan to my wife, and I told her that since we don't have a baby yet, we should have just rent a smaller unit or even rent a room to lower down our expenses. And, we should rent out our beloved unit now," he said. "I wonder what happens next" I grinned. "You guess it right. It was just like an earthquake. We argued for almost a month before we settle down with some agreement. She agreed to rent out our beloved unit and rented another master bedroom for own stay. She even gave me a 3 years deadline. If I am not doing well, I have to drop my plan and go back to current state" he said. "I guess you succeeded," I said. "Correct" he grinned. John then shared the numbers when he rents out his entire apartment.

	Current State	Proposal
Property Price	RM400K	RM400K
Loan amount	RM360K	RM360K
Loan interest rate	4.20%	4.20%
Loan tenure	40 years	40 years
Monthly instalment	RM1,550	RM1,550
Rental Income		RM1,600

Rental payable		RM400
Net Profit	-RM1,550	-RM350

"So, you are actually putting RM1,200 per month into your pocket after that?" I asked. "Yes, and that will accelerate my progress in accumulating cash and regain back my loan eligibility," he said. "I believe nothing can stop you on purchasing new properties after that," I said. "Yes, even since, I purchased 5 more properties, and those properties generated approximately RM1,500 passive income every month," he said. "And then, you can use that passive income to pay off your monthly installment?" I asked. "That's right. It really seems like someone is helping me to pay off my housing loan and I am staying for free" he said. "I guess it also happened in the current unit you are staying?" I asked. "You guess it right." he grinned.

Before we head to bed, John provided a few guidelines:

1. Never buy and stay if this is your first property
2. If you are getting debts, make sure someone pays it for you
3. Start early. It will take more effort when you have kids

6. Make Sure Someone Pays Off Your Debts

One day, after dinner together with John, we have another chit-chat session. "Hey John, how long have you been investing in the property market?" I asked. "It has been almost 8 years. I started when I came back from Singapore 8 years ago" he answered. "No wonder you can acquire so many properties. I believe this is because of your savings while you are working in Singapore" I said. "Nope, that's not true; all I have saved is the amount of money which is sufficient to pay the down payment for the first property. If I was working in Malaysia, I believe if I spent wisely, I would have saved that amount of money also" he clarified. "So, what happened? Why don't you make any significant savings while you were in Singapore?" I asked. "That is because I visited Marina Bay Sand too frequent. Luckily Penang is far away from Genting Highlands, and my gambling desire is not strong enough till I willing to travel all the way down to Genting" he laughed.

Derrick Jonathan

In one of the drink session with John, he emphasized the beauty of getting others to pay off your debts. Mortgage interests are extremely expensive. When you look at the loan payment details, you will observe that big chunk of the payment is actually paying off the mortgage interest instead of the principal. He then showed me the principal and interest payment of a RM400K property with RM40K down payment, 4.2% interest rate, and 40 years loan tenure.

Years	Principal	Interest	Balance
1st	Rm3,544	Rm15,052	Rm356,456
2nd	Rm7,239	Rm29,953	Rm352,761
3rd	Rm11,093	Rm44,695	Rm348,907
4th	Rm15,111	Rm59,273	Rm344,889
5th	Rm19,302	Rm73,678	Rm340,698

Based on the numbers, immediately you will notice that the mortgage interests are huge. John told us that if you have to take on debts, make sure someone else pays for it. The only recommended solution is to rent out your unit. However, he also mentioned if you want to be successful in renting out your unit, there are few guidelines that might be beneficial to us.

Buy and Rent Guidelines:

Rule 1. Believe in buy and rent strategy

Rule 2. Never rent out empty unit

Rule 3. Buy apartment with a high occupancy rate

Rule 4. Don't overspend in renovation

Rule 5. Act fast

After John listed down all the guidelines, he clearly explained why those guidelines are important, and he provided examples on most of them.

Rule 1. Believe in buy and rent strategy

Whatever you are doing, you need to have faith in your strategy. You will never achieve success if you think it is impossible. Buy and rent strategy might sound impossible to some people, but those who do it before will know how easy it is to buy and rent if you know the tricks. Do not listen to those who never do this before; consult those who have bought and rented out more than 5 properties.

You might have pulled back in the past when you heard people discuss haunted property, unreasonable tenants, inconsistent rental payment, property damaged by tenant, tenant commit suicide at a rented unit, etc. To be frank, bad things do happen, but the occurrence rate is very low. It might only happen at 1 out of 1,000 rented properties. Why bother? Why focus on the low occurrence excursions? If you are so unlucky, if bad things really happen to you, I am sure you and everyone else can figure out a way to deal with it.

John mentioned that if you want to minimize the risk of getting poor tenants, you can be extra cautious when selecting a tenant. Few things he proposes us to check-

How many tenants will be staying together?

Limit the number of tenants. Higher number of tenants will end up higher damage to your property. Meanwhile, you will need to be careful if they have small kids. You won't like them to treat your nicely painted wall as drawing paper.

Do they have a regular paycheck?

You might want to check whether they are self-employed or employed. It is preferable to rent out for employed professional as they have a regular paycheck and you can expect consistent payment from them. Never rent out to those that cannot explain their job functions clearly. The possibility is high that they are jobless and will drag their rental payment.

How long they will be staying?

It is preferable to have a tenancy agreement for more than 1 year. You would not want to repeat the process of getting a new tenant unless your short-term tenant agrees to pay with higher rental fees. Sometimes, the tenant may not be honest how long they will be staying; you might want to test them out by telling them that their 2 months rental deposit will be forfeited if they stay less than 1 year. If they started to show anger, the possibility is high that they don't plan to stay long. For those who plan to stay for long, they won't care anyway. So, never afraid that you will scare tenants away if you tested them.

Do they have clean and neat attire?

If they take care of their attire, it is most likely they will take care of your unit also. If you don't want your unit to become a dog house, make sure you don't rent to those that don't take care of their own attire.

Rule 2. Never rent out empty unit

John told us that there are two disadvantages to renting out empty unit. Typically, if you try to rent out empty unit, it will take time to attract tenants, and the rental income is significantly lower too. In the current Penang property market, the rental supply is higher than the rental demand. In other words, the tenant has more choices, and they will certainly go for a unit which has a lower rental and better condition. If your unit is unfurnished or poorly renovated, it is very hard to attract their attention. At the end of the day, if you insist on renting out your empty unit, you will have to lower your rent. Hence, it is not recommended to rent out empty unit because financially you will do poorer. John gave an example also regarding this point.

	Empty Unit	Fully furnished
Property Price	RM400K	RM400K
Renovation fees		RM10K
Rental per month	RM1K	RM1.3K
Months before rent out	4	1
Income after 5 years	+RM56K (56mths rental income)	+RM67K (59mths rental income)

Referring to his example, you will notice that in the longer term, you will earn more if you renovated and furnished your unit. Apart from that, you will be able to sell your property at a higher price as you will definitely have a higher demand with the better-looking unit.

Rule 3. Buy apartment with a high occupancy rate

John explained that your rental income very much depends on the demand of your unit. If your unit is located at a strategic location with a high occupancy rate, your unit will most probably take up faster with higher rental income. Thus, high occupancy rate is very crucial during property hunting.

There are a few ways to determine the occupancy rate-

1. Visit the apartment or condominium at night time and look at how many units have lights turn on, probably in between 9pm till 10pm when everyone returns home after working or dinner. If most of the lights were on, the occupancy rate is high. It is preferable to do it during weekdays as some of the residents might go back to their hometown during the weekend.

2. Pay close attention to the balcony. If the unit is occupied, you might find traces of gardening or laundry activities. This is not as accurate as the first method as most of the youngsters nowadays use a dryer to dry their clothes and it is difficult to track when the residents will do their laundry.

3. Inspect the number of cars at the carpark. If carpark is fully occupied, it means the occupancy is high. For open carpark, you have to be extra cautious as those cars might belong to nearby residents.

Rule 4. Don't overspend in renovation

Rule 2 taught us not to rent out empty unit while Rule 4 suggested not to overdo on your renovation. Your rental income will not increase limitlessly if you put more money in renovating your unit. In other words, your unit might be able to rent out 20%-30% higher rental, but it is impossible to rent out 2 times higher rental no matter how you beautify your unit. In renovating your property, John advised us to use a minimalist concept. The renovation work needs to be simple; the design needs to be neat and tidy. The key focus is to make the unit feel spacious, tidy and comfortable. Besides, minimalist concept also helps to control renovation expenses. To better justify his concept, John showed us some numbers again.

	Fancy Renovation	Minimalist renovation
Property Price	RM400K	RM400K
Renovation fees	RM50K	RM10K
Rental per month	RM1.5K	RM1.3K
Income after 5 years	+RM40K	+RM68K

Rule 5. Act fast

As John mentioned multiple times, time is our biggest enemy. This is especially true for property investment. You will have to engage multiple parties to help you up with all the execution. This includes property agents, lawyers, bankers, and other relevant professionals. You shouldn't delay your key collection, your renovation works and renting out your unit. John told me that it takes him about 1-2 months to rent out his unit after key collection. He also mentioned that he would start hunting furniture prior to key collection. Some of the owners will drag up to 1 year to finish up everything. That will put them into very poor financial position. John's example below should more than RM15K different if you are able to rent out at a faster pace. In order to act fast, you will have to delegate your tasks correctly to professionals; able to make fast and accurate decision; and keep track on the overall schedule.

	John	Other Owners
Property Price	RM400K	RM400K
Renovation fees	RM10K	RM10K
Rental per month	RM1.3K	RM1.3K
Months before rent out	1	12
Income after 5 years	+RM67K (59mths rental income)	+RM52.4K (48mths rental income)

7. Follow the Game Rules

I have been working as a product engineer for the past 5 years. My current job role is to qualify and release new products to the production run. There are a number of product qualification to run before we sign off to release the new products. Product qualification includes Burn-In, Split lot analysis, product characteristic, etc. One day, I was so frustrated at the number of works to be completed before we can qualify a new product. I waived some of the product qualification activities and released that new product to production. Unexpectedly, after 1 month into production, the product suffered massive low yield due to the waiver I made one month ago. At the end of the day, we have to decommit our customer deliveries and re-qualify that particular product. My direct supervisor gave me a half-day lecture on the criticalness to follow the product qualification rules. I admitted my mistake and promised to strictly follow the rules no matter what happens.

At the remaining working hours, I was thinking quite a lot about following the rules. Suddenly, I found a missing puzzle on property investment. I couldn't recall John ever told me about how to counter the government rules which curb property speculation. I was pretty sure that the bank would only approve a maximum 70% loan to value for residential units if the buyer has more than 2 residential units with loan. If this is true, how could John acquire 15 properties in such a short term?

That night, I plan to pay John another visit to understand this. "Hey John, do you know there is a restriction that buyer can only get a maximum 70% loan to value if he or she has more than 2 residential units with loans?" I asked. "Sure do. But that is not really some blocking point" he answered. "Why it is not the obstacle?" I asked. "Well, there are some tricks to counter it" he answered. "Is it legal?" I asked. "Of course, there are so many ways to earn money legally, why risk yourself with illegal way?" he smiled. John explained that there are two simple ways to acquire more properties even with that restriction.

1. Form investment pool
2. negotiate with the seller to get a significant discount on the down payment. 30% or more is not a myth

Form investment pool

John told us that forming an investment pool is difficult that he can imagine. You need to have a strong desire to be successful in creating an investment pool. He mentioned that he encountered a lot of hiccups when he is leading the investment pool. Most of the arguments were caused by different opinions and lack of co-operation or collaboration among the team. Based on his past learning, he provided us with 6 major steps that we have to follow through in order to achieve a higher success rate. He reminded us that we have to follow through those 6 steps in the correct sequence. The six major steps include forming a team; arranging a viewing and shortlisting properties; further discussion on shortlisted properties; make a decision on which to buy and which to keep in view; execute based on decision made; review, revise to improve future doing and repeat the property acquisition process.

Six major steps to form an investment group

1. Form a team
2. Arrange viewing and shortlisting
3. Meet up to discuss
4. Make a fast decision

5. Execute

6. Review, revise and recreate

1. Form a team

This is the most important step. You will have to form a diversified team to be effective and efficient. Preferably, you need to have someone who is familiar with legal stuff, someone who is good in ROI calculation, someone who is good in shortlisting good property, someone who is good in negotiation and finally someone who is good in collaboration. Everyone will have to play their parts accordingly. Apart from the special skill sets, team members will need to fulfill certain requirements which are able to contribute to the investment pool. Their requirements include loan eligibility, investment cash or 90% loan-to-value quota. It is less beneficial if you recruit someone who has none of those requirements as they can't help much in growing the investment pool. After you identify the potential team members, you will have to arrange a few meet up to make sure everyone gets to know each other and have basic trust. In this stage, you will have to let go of someone who makes others feel uncomfortable. It will be much more difficult to do so if you already started the investment pool.

Once the team members are finalized, it is time to discuss everyone contribution. Preferably, everyone should contribute the same amount of money to the investment pool. For those who contributed either the loan eligibility or 90% loan-to-value quota, they should have higher profit sharing on that particular property. The main reason to have an equal amount of cash investment is to ensure everyone has similar exposure to profit and loss.

2. Arrange viewing and shortlisting

The next step is to arrange viewing and shortlisting. Preferably, there is someone who is good at identifying the good unit to invest among team members. He or she will be responsible for gathering the requirements from team members and identify the suitable units from property websites or from property agents. The property requirements normally include property type; property price; property size; number of bedroom and bathroom and capacity of the carpark. Typically, it is good to give a range to be more efficient. John provided us with an example on how his team is doing this.

Property requirements:

1. Property price: RM100K – RM200K

2. Property type: apartment or condominium

3. Property size: > 700sqf

4. Bedroom and Bathroom: > 2 bedrooms

5. Carpark: 1

Once the team defined the requirements, he or she will identify suitable units from property website or send these requirements to property agents to look for suitable units. There are few property websites in Malaysia which provides a good database for screening. This includes property guru, iproperty and mudah.

Popular property websites-

- Propertyguru website- www.propertyguru.com.my

- Iproperty website- www.iproperty.com.my

- Mudah website- www.mudah.my

After shortlisting suitable properties, viewing will be arranged. Viewing date will send to all team members, and you will have to strongly encourage all team members to attend the viewing session as this will help them to make a decision in the later stage. During the viewing session, everyone will jot down the pros and cons for all units. Preferably, no one should make comments during the viewing session as this might influence others. Discussion should be done after viewing is completed.

3. Meet up and discuss

After all suitable units have been viewed, the leader will have to schedule a meet up to discuss the outcome from the viewing. Everyone takes a turn to share their opinions. The leader needs to make sure everyone has their chance to voice out their concerns, and no one from the team should dominate the discussion. This will make sure everyone participates, and no one will be disappointed or blamed each other after the decision is made. In this stage, the team needs to calculate the return on investment based on the expected capital appreciation and rental yield.

John recommended that good deals typically have ROI more than 2x. ROI calculation is very critical as this is the main factor to decide whether to buy or drop. Due to the criticalness, it is always recommended to have few people to check the ROI computation. You will need to pay penalty fees if you revert your decision after you make a booking. In the event that consensus cannot be reached, voting is necessary.

4. Make a fast decision

Good deals won't last long. The process of viewing, shortlisting and analyzing should be done as soon as possible. Bargain buys normally will attract a lot of potential buyers, and it might sell out within a few days. That is the reason why decision making needs to be fast to avoid disappointment. Preferably, viewing, shorting, analyzing and making judgment call should be done less than 1 week. When the team gets more mature, when everyone has mutual trust among each other, the cycle time normally will greatly reduce. John told us that the normal cycle time his team is doing currently is less than 3days. There are less meet up, and they normally make the decision using WhatsApp or emails.

5. Execute

Plans are only good intentions unless they immediately degenerate into hard work. After all the planning works, you will have to continue with execution. In this stage, someone with good negotiation and collaboration skills is important. He or she will have to negotiate with sellers, property agents, lawyers and bankers to reduce the purchase price or professional fees. Meanwhile, he or she has to also collaborate and follow up closely on all activities.

Execution includes paying an earnest deposit to property agent or seller; applying for a housing loan with bankers; selecting best matching loan contract; engage with a lawyer on SPA and LA signing and finally follow up on bank loan release and key collection. It is very time consuming and tiring work. To better appreciate the efforts given by the executor, John suggested that the executor should have higher profit sharing, preferably 5-10% higher. John mentioned that his team is giving up 10% higher profit sharing to his executor as he is the one doing all the works.

6. Review, revise and recreate

John reminded us that the last step is very critical. Most team has forgotten to have proper closure. The closure is very important because the team can only improve when they relook back into the whole process; they just went through and provided feedback or comments on what went right and what went wrong. This will prevent the team from making the same mistake and will improve the team operation efficiencies. Review and revise is not necessary to carry out only at the end of the process. In every stage, whenever it is necessary, periodic review and revise is good to have. After proper closure, the team can move on to the next purchase, and they have to repeat step 1 to step 6 again. Prior to that, the team need to check their cash balance, remaining loan eligibility and remaining 90% loan-to-value quota. That will help to define the target.

At the end of the discussion, John reminded me again that forming an investment group is not a straight forward activity. You might encounter some obstacles before you can be successful. Nevertheless, if you follow the step by step guidance provided by him, your success rate will be much higher. At least, that is what is happening on the property investment team that he is currently coaching.

Negotiate with the seller to get a significant discount on down payment

Apart from forming an investment pool, John also taught us to negotiate with the seller to get significant discount on down payment. He emphasized that down payment discount more than 30% is not a myth. According to him, most of the units that his investment group is acquiring recently has more than 30% down payment discount. It is not easy for normal people to identify those great deals. However, if you are able to inspect properties under John's lens, you will probably have a higher chance to find them. Based on his experience, there are very high possibilities that you can successfully negotiate to reduce the down payment for units which are unsold for a long time, units which belong to desperate seller and seller who is keen to negotiate.

1. Good unit unsold for a long time

Typically, you will find this unit through property website or through your own inspection at certain area. You will less likely hear this from property agents because they might already feel tired promoting those units. You might notice them appear in property website for a few months and the price was reduced from months to months. You might also notice them when you are performing inspection at a certain area. The "For Sale" advertisement posters might have worn out or dropped on the floor. Those are some of the signs that those units were remained unsold for quite some time.

There are various reasons why those units remained unsold. Most probably the price was set too high, or the unit was in very poor condition. If you found those units, you will have a higher chance that seller will reduce the down payment as they might think that the demand is low and they grab any opportunity they have. You might want to be extra cautious before you acquire those units. There might be a valid reason why there were unsold for so long. There might be a haunted unit; there might be no clear title; there might be some troublesome tenants who refuse to move out, etc. Once you understand the reason, and you think you can solve those issues, those units are definitely something you should consider.

2. Desperate seller

Desperate sellers are normally more open for discussion. They might want to sell off their property as they might need cash urgently. Typically, you will get to know this kind of deal from both property agents and property websites. Those sellers normally offer much higher agent fees to encourage property agents. If you receive similar proposals from a few agents, normally this indicates that the proposed unit is urgently for sale. Meanwhile, if you notice many property agents are posting the similar unit at property websites, that also indicates the seller is very desperate. Similarly, you will have to verify what's the root cause of urgent sales. If it is nothing to do with the property itself, those units are good deals.

3. Seller who is keen to negotiate

John reminded us that most of the properties listed for sales are price negotiable. Even though some of them insist that the price is not negotiable when the deal is about to close they might be able to reduce another RM5K – RM10K. Always remember to negotiate for a price reduction. Even the amount might not be significant; it is definitely better than nothing. Some sellers are very keen on price negotiation. You might notice from property websites that some sellers will state clearly the selling price is negotiable. In general, this type of sellers will list their properties with higher selling price with the hope that someone will take it out with a higher price. On the other hand, these sellers are also uncertain what should be the correct selling price. With good negotiation and the right amount of pressure, they will reduce their selling price significantly. These reductions might go into down payment discount.

8. 200% ROI WITHIN 5 YEARS IS NOT A MYTH

After spending so many nights with John, I pretty sure I pick up most of the skillsets to be successful in property investment. By now, I know how to accurately calculate the return on investment, how to improve the return on investment, how to negotiate to reduce down payment, how to identify the suitable unit to buy, etc.

There is one thing that I wasn't that sure till now. Although we spent nights discussing on how to calculate and improve ROI. I still don't see there is any possibility to get a 200% ROI within 5 years. This is one of the criteria that John kept emphasizing that we should only acquire properties that will give us a 200% ROI. However, the examples that John gave previously were well below 2x.

"Hey John, there is something that bothers me," I told John one day after our dinner. "Well, go straight to your question please" he replied. "You know, when you are teaching me how to calculate and improve ROI, you gave a few examples. The ROI within 5 years for those examples were well below 2x. And, you also told me that I should only acquire property which will give us ROI more than 2 times within 5 years. I was afraid I don't know the tricks to achieve that yet" I said.

"Oh, it's that true. I haven't told you anything about the four property investments myth yet?" he asked. "I guess not, what's so interesting about those four myths?" I asked. "Those are your breakthroughs to acquire properties which give you ROI > 2x within 5 years," he said. "Go ahead. I am listening" I said.

"The main reason why it seems to be difficult to most people because they are holding on some myths which are not valid," he said. "The four myths include rental yield will never be above 8%; annual capital appreciation will never be above 10%; ROI within 5 years will never be above > 2x and down payment must be above 10%" he continued.

"So, are you saying that we need to have rental yield more than 8%, annual capital appreciation more than 10% or down payment less than 10% in order to achieve ROI more than 2x within 5 years?" I asked. "Not entirely true, but you will have a higher chance to achieve ROI more than 2x within 5 years if you can beat those myths" he answered.

Looking back into the previous notes, return on investment is driven by income and expenses. In other words, if you can increase your income and lower down your expenses, you can improve your return on investment. According to John, the first three myths are related to increasing income and the fourth myth is related to cost reduction.

Property investment myths-

Myth1: Rental yield will never be above 8%

Myth2: Annual capital appreciation will never be above 10%

Myth3: ROI within 5 years will never be above 2x

Myth4: down payment must be above 10%

Myth1: Rental yield will never be above 8%

The typical rental yield in Penang is less than 4%. That doesn't mean that you won't be able to get a rental yield above 8%. There are a few ways you can achieve that. Rental yield is basically calculated based on annual rental income divided by the property purchase price. Hence, to increase rental yield, you either have to increase your rental income or reduce your property purchase price.

Take RM150K property, for example; the monthly rental is RM500 for a rental yield of 4%. To increase the rental yield from 4% to 8%, you just need to increase your monthly rental RM300-RM400 and reduce your purchase price to RM120K-RM135K. John said that it is not as difficult as you think, but it is easier to achieve with lower priced property in Penang. Rental income can be improved through proper renovation and furnishing while property price can be reduced through negotiations with sellers.

	Typical	Improve1	Improve2
Mthly Rental	500	900	800
Property Price	150000	135000	120000
Rental Yield	4.00%	8.00%	8.00%

Myth2: Annual capital appreciation will never be above 10%

The typical capital appreciation is about 7% in Penang. Nevertheless, capital appreciation of more than 10% is achievable. Similar to rental yield, John taught us to breakdown on the items which affect capital appreciation. Annual capital appreciation is computed based on the average incremental price per year. For example, if property increases from 150K to 200K within 5 years, the annual capital appreciation is 5.9%.

Annual Capital appreciation = $(200/150)^{(1/5)}$ = 1.059 (5.9%)

Based on the formula for annual capital appreciation, there are two options to improve annual capital appreciation. It is either to reduce the purchase price or to increase the selling price. John said this is really easy to achieve. All you have to do is to reduce your purchase price by 10% and increase your selling price by 10%. While comparing the overall impact on reducing purchase price and increasing selling price, 20% reduction at a purchase price (Improve2) has 1% higher annual capital appreciation than 20% increment at selling price. To have a higher success rate, negotiate to purchase at a lower price is more important.

	Typical	Improve 1	Improve 2	Improve3
Purchase Price	150,000	135,000	120,000	150,000
Selling Price after 5 years	210,383	231,421	210,383	252,460
Annual Capital Appreciation	7%	11%	12%	11%

Myth3: ROI within 5 years will never be above 2x

If you are able to breakthrough myth1 and myth2, you will most likely able to overcome myth3. Using a similar example, John plugged in numbers for a typical scenario and improved scenario. In typical scenario, he used 7% annual capital appreciation and 4% rental yield while at an improved scenario, he used 10% annual capital appreciation and 8% rental yield. Keeping the expenses to be the same, ROI within 5 years will increase from 1.30x to 2.17x.

John reminded us that this computation was assuming that the expenses are expected to keep stagnant. In fact, in myth4, he will disclose how exactly you can further reduce your expenses and further improve the ROI within 5 years.

	Typical	Improved
Capital Appreciation	RM60,383 (7%)	RM91,577 (10%)
Rental Income	RM30,000 (4%)	RM60,000 (8%)
Income in 5 years	RM90,383	RM151,577
Down payment	RM15,000 (10.0%)	RM15,000 (10.0%)
Agent Fees	Buy: RM1,500 Rent: RM5,000	Buy: RM1,500 Rent: RM5,000
Legal Fees and Stamp Duty	Stamp duty: RM2,750 Legal Fees: RM1,500	Stamp duty: RM2,750 Legal Fees: RM1,500
Maintenance Fees and Sinking Fund	RM4,500 (5 years)	RM4,500 (5 years)
Quit Rent and Assessment Fees	RM1,100 (5 years)	RM1,100 (5 years)
Renovation and Furnishing Fees	RM10,000	RM10,000
Mortgage Interests in 5 years	RM28,437 (5 years, RM150K, 4.4%)	RM28,437 (5 years, RM150K, 4.4%)
Expenses in 5 years	RM69,787	RM69,787

ROI in 5 years	1.30x	2.17x

Myth4: down payment must be above 10%

Typically, whenever you purchase a property, you have to pay a minimum 10% down payment for a residential unit and a minimum 15% down payment for a commercial unit. If you have more than 2 residential units with loans, you will have to pay a minimum 30% down payment for a residential unit. Nevertheless, John told us that this is not always mandatory. Sometimes, you should be able to reduce your down payment and keep cash for future purposes.

The easiest way is to purchase new property directly from a developer who offers down payment rebate. Due to the slow property market, some of the developers will even give you zero down payment offer. John told us that you could do this trick at sub-sales too. If you are acquiring a RM150K apartment, you are supposed to pay RM15K as a down payment to the seller and apply for RM135K loan from the bank.

To reduce down payment, you can ask a seller to reduce the RM15K down payment and continue to apply for RM135K loan and putting RM150K property selling price in sales and purchase agreement. John reminded us that we have to check with an appointed lawyer on this type of down payment reduction to make sure you do not break any rules and regulations. There are so many ways to earn money, never ever use an illegal method.

Real-life examples from John

John explained the four myths very thoroughly, but I was still not 100% convinced that those are really achievable. It did sound like it is not totally impossible now, but I would like to have some real-life examples from John. He noticed that I am still very doubtful about what I have been told. After some hesitation, he decided to share me 3 real examples.

Example1: 15% down payment where 5% use for renovation

In 2010, John bought an apartment at Jalan Batu Uban, Penang. Market value was about RM300K. He was able to negotiate with the seller and bought it with a 15% discount. The actual purchase price was RM255K, and the selling price was RM300K on paper. In other words, he doesn't have to pay even 1cent for down payment, and he got RM15K cash back when bank loan release. He then used the

RM15K for renovation which eventually caused him RM10K.

Although the market is very slow from 2010 to 2015, as that apartment is very nearby University Science Malaysia, the capital appreciation is slightly better than average. The market value increased to RM400K. The rental yield is about 5.2%, RM1,300 per month, slightly higher than normal rate as the unit was renovated and fully furnished. The ROI within 5 years for this example1 is 2.59x.

	Example1
Capital Appreciation	RM145,000
Rental Income	RM78,000
Cash Back	RM5,000
Income in 5 years	RM228,000
Down payment	RM0
Agent Fees	Buy: RM3,000 Rent: RM7,500
Legal Fees and Stamp Duty	Stamp duty: RM6,350 Legal Fees: RM3,000
Maintenance Fees and Sinking Fund	RM9,000 (5 years)
Quit Rent and Assessment Fees	RM2,250 (5 years)

Renovation and Furnishing Fees	RM0
Mortgage Interests in 5 years	RM56,875 (5 years, RM270K, 4.4%)
Expenses in 5 years	RM87,975
ROI in 5 years	2.59x

Example2: 10% down payment reduction on renovated unit

In 2012, John and his team bought one apartment at Bayan Baru. It was renovated and fully furnished unit. Market value was RM250K, and the deal was signed at a 10% discount which is RM225K. Discount was again given directly on a down payment. Loan amount was RM225K. No renovation cost as the unit was in good shape.

Five years later, the market value increases to RM320K. In between, he rented out with a rental yield of about 5.0%, RM950 per month. The ROI within 5 years for example2 is 2.13x.

	Example2
Capital Appreciation	RM95,000
Rental Income	RM57,000
Income in 5 years	RM152,000

Down payment	RM0
Agent Fees	Buy: RM2,500 Rent: RM4,500
Legal Fees and Stamp Duty	Stamp duty: RM5,125 Legal Fees: RM2,500
Maintenance Fees and Sinking Fund	RM7,500 (5 years)
Quit Rent and Assessment Fees	RM1,875 (5 years)
Renovation and Furnishing Fees	RM0
Mortgage Interests in 5 years	RM47,396 (5 years, RM225K, 4.4%)
Expenses in 5 years	71396
ROI in 5 years	2.13x

Example3: Buying in tourist attraction area, use it as Airbnb

Penang is always famous as tourist attraction spot. In 2013, John purchased one apartment at Batu Ferringhi and rent it out using Airbnb platform. He delegated the Airbnb management to one property agent, in exchange he gave 30% of the total Airbnb revenue to that property agent. He bought that unit directly from a developer with a purchase price of RM1 Million. It was zero down payment unit, and all the legal fees and stamp duty was waived. He applied loan for the remaining RM900K. He spent about

RM30K for renovation and furnishing. It is higher than usual as he needs to beautify the unit to attract Airbnb tenants. After deducting the Airbnb management fees, he was earning about RM5K per month. At the end of 2017, the market value for that luxury apartment was RM1.3 Million. The ROI within 5 years for example3 is 2.73x.

	Example3
Capital Appreciation	RM400,000
Rental Income	RM300,000
Income in 5 years	RM700,000
Down payment	RM0
Agent Fees	Buy: RM0 (Direct developer) Rent: RM0 (Airbnb management)
Legal Fees and Stamp Duty	Stamp duty: Waived Legal Fees: Waived
Maintenance Fees and Sinking Fund	RM30,000 (5 years)
Quit Rent and Assessment Fees	RM7,500 (5 years)

Renovation and Furnishing Fees	30000
Mortgage Interests in 5 years	RM189,582 (5 years, RM225K, 4.4%)
Expenses in 5 years	RM257,082
ROI in 5 years	2.73x

Epilogue

Congratulations if you make it this far. You are one more step closer to financial freedom through property investment. Till now, you should have equipped yourselves with all the necessary skill sets and knowledge to be successful in property investment. Before you challenge yourselves in a real market, John told us a few more tips which are extremely useful when you further progress in the future. For property investment, it is possible to earn money through property flipping, but it is nearly impossible to earn serious money by doing short term. You will significantly increase your expenses if you do so. Additional expenses include RPGT (Real Property Gain Tax), bank penalty, agent fees, legal fees, etc. It is those that stay long enough in the game which will enjoy the max profit.

John recommended us to buy, rent and hold for at least 5 years. The best scenario is to sell only after the property price double. Buy, sell and buy again not only make you lose money from extra agent fees, stamp duty, legal fees, it will also be very time-consuming. Instead of doing property flipping, you would better to spend your time doing something else or look for additional property units to invest. Don't ever get emotional in a hot market or slow market. Stay calm and let the money grow itself.

Property investment is not a gambling or stock market which will give you high returns in very short time frame. It is almost like the index fund which gradually increases in longer horizon. John reminded us to be very patient and never ever underestimate what you can achieve in the long term. Although stock market annual increment is likely to be higher than property market, at the end of the day, you might earn even more for property investment because you can leverage your debts and you can earn extra from rental income.

Leveraging debts simply means that if you have RM10K cash, you can purchase RM100K property while you can only invest RM10K in the stock market. If both the property market and stock market increase in similar rate, you will earn RM7K from property market and only RM700 from the stock market. Although you have to pay other fees for acquiring property, in the end, you will still earn higher in property investment. However, John did not recommend us to put all our money into property investment.

The best way is to have a balanced portfolio where you have property, stock, and bond investment together. If your intention is to achieve financial freedom through property investment, you will need to do your math carefully. You have to calculate how many properties you have to acquire to provide you with a sufficient passive income to cover your daily expenses. You need to set a clear goal, develop your plan, follow through carefully and revise your plan if necessary.

John emphasized that we have to start taking actions. Single action taken is better than ten well-developed plans. However, whatever you are doing in property investment, it is always good to calculate the potential and risk before you sign a deal. You have to be consistent with what you are doing. Don't get impatient or emotional. On the other hand, don't be too cautious or picky and keep waiting for the best one to come. You won't be buying only one, why bother to get the lowest priced unit. As long as it meets your ROI goal, you are good to go. Don't forget that time is always your biggest enemy. Due to less experience or exposure, you might not succeed on your first few units. However, don't give up. You will eventually pick up the right rhythm, and you will be financial free progressively. Be brave; make your very first step earlier. Typically, the very first step is the most difficult to make. Once you get started, it will be a lot easier. Do not afraid of failures, get up and repeat the process again. The more you fail, the more success you will be.

About the Author

Derrick Jonathan has been working as an engineer for more than 15 years. He understands that it is extremely difficult to achieve financial freedom solely with employed income. He always keeps an open mind and challenges the normal way of doing this, including property investment. He holds Master Degree of Business Administration, Bachelor Degree of Engineering, Six Sigma Black Belt and Project Management Professional. He is a successful property investor and advisor, a successful business coach who help to bring up businesses including a cafe, online shop, legal firm, etc. He founded and own businesses including a cafe, business consultant, property investment, etc.

He fought and argued that not only the rich one can profit from the property market. Any people with different background and income level can benefit from property investment. He provided simple steps to increase your chances to excel in property investment. As he shared the lesson learned from his friend, John, you will get to understand the fundamental easier, and it helps you to apply in your real-life hunting.

www.ingramcontent.com/pod-product-compliance
Lightning Source LLC
Chambersburg PA
CBHW030657220526
45463CB00005B/1815